Craven-Pamlico-Carteret
Regional Library

D1399803

WONDERS OF ALASKA

NORTH TO ALASKA

Lynn M. Stone

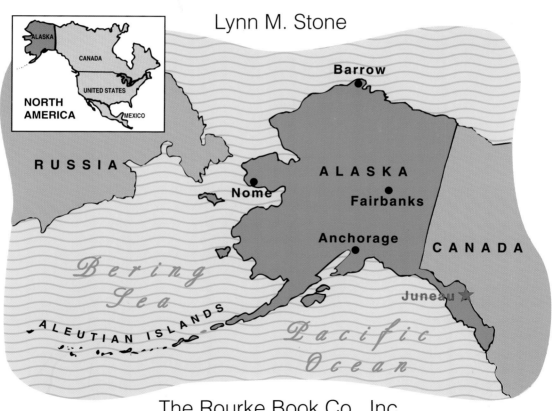

The Rourke Book Co., Inc.
Vero Beach, Florida 32964

Craven–Pamlico–Carteret
Regional Library

© 1994 The Rourke Book Co., Inc.

All rights reserved. No part of this book may be reproduced or utilized in any form or by any means, electronic or mechanical including photocopying, recording or by any information storage and retrieval system without permission in writing from the publisher.

Edited by Sandra A. Robinson

PHOTO CREDITS
Courtesy Alaska Division of Tourism: pages 8, 12, 15, 18, 21; courtesy ARCO: page 7; © Lynn M. Stone: cover, title page, pages 4, 10, 13, 17

Library of Congress Cataloging-in-Publication Data

Stone, Lynn M.
    Wonders of Alaska / Lynn M. Stone
    p. cm. — (North to Alaska)
    Includes index.
    ISBN 1-55916-028-4
    1. Alaska—Description and travel—Juvenile literature.
[1. Alaska—Description and travel.] I. Title. II. Series: Stone, Lynn M. North to Alaska.
F904.3.S77 1994
917.9804'5–dc20   93-42648
                                  CIP

Printed in the USA   AC

c.001

TABLE OF CONTENTS

WONDERS OF ALASKA

Alaska is not just the United States' 49th and largest state. It is a northern land of adventure, mystery and, most of all, wonder. Almost nothing in Alaska is ordinary.

Alaskans and visitors alike find that the state's wonders are unending. Each day in Alaska offers something new, surprising, wonderful!

Alaska's wildlife and rugged beauty are natural wonders — but Alaskans themselves have created a few wonders, too.

One of Alaska's natural wonders, an Alaska brown bear, hikes toward another wonder, a distant glacier

TRANS-ALASKA PIPELINE

One of the wonders built by Alaskans is the Trans-Alaska Pipeline. "Trans" means "across." Completed in the 1970s, the pipeline transports oil across Alaska 800 miles south from Prudhoe Bay to the seaport of Valdez.

The pipeline is a wonder of careful planning and construction. Wrapped in heavy insulation, or cover against the cold, the pipeline travels over rivers, through mountain ranges and above frozen ground.

The Trans-Alaska Pipeline snakes southward from Prudhoe Bay in northern Alaska

IDITAROD SLED DOG RACE

Each March brings excitement to Alaskans. The Iditarod Sled Dog Race, a wonder of strength and courage, begins.

Alaska's best dog teams and their **mushers,** or drivers, race in the two-week-long Iditarod. The Iditarod Trail stretches 1,049 miles from Anchorage to Nome. Imagine traveling that distance by dog sled!

Nighttime temperatures can feel like 100 degrees below zero. No wonder the Iditarod is called The Last Great Race!

Out on the trail, a musher barks orders at his team of sled dogs

ALASKA RAILROAD

The Alaska Railroad is like no other railroad in the United States. It is the only railroad with freight and passenger service operated, or run, by a state government. It is also the only American railroad that regularly makes "flag stops."

A flag stop occurs if someone along the tracks waves for the train to stop. Hunters, fishermen and cold, lost hikers in the woods have been helped — even saved — by Alaska Railroad trains.

The railroad operates about 500 miles of track, mostly between Seward, Anchorage and Fairbanks.

Alaska Railroad trains rumble through some of America's most scenic country

Alaska's "midnight sun" shines behind whalebone in an Eskimo village

*Alaska's wild wonders — a bald eagle
perched near wildflowers on a seaside ledge*

ALASKA MARINE HIGHWAY

The Alaska Marine Highway is a sheltered waterway along the coast of Southeast Alaska.

The Marine Highway is also called the Inside Passage. Ferryboats sail the "inner" side of islands that shelter ships from the open sea.

The ferries travel to Alaskan ports from Seattle, Washington, and towns in British Columbia, Canada.

Green forests, glaciers, snowy mountains, eagles and **pods** of whales make the Passage a traveler's dream.

A cruise ship in Glacier Bay on the Alaska Marine Highway

McNEIL RIVER STATE GAME SANCTUARY

More brown, or grizzly, bears gather at the McNeil River State Game Sanctuary than at any other one place on Earth. Sometimes as many as 80 bears fish for salmon here at the same time. Part of the wonder is that *people* are here with them.

Each summer day a small, lucky group of people is chosen to hike to the falls. Up close, the visitors to the bears' home quietly watch the big "brownies" fish.

Jaws locked on its prize salmon, a brown bear splashes ashore from the McNeil River

MOUNT McKINLEY

Mount McKinley, in south central Alaska, is the highest peak in North America. Mount McKinley towers 20,320 feet above **sea level.** The mountain was named for President William McKinley (1897-1901).

Mount McKinley is cold, windy and rugged. Many climbers have died on its slopes.

The Athabaskans, some of Alaska's first people, called the mountain "Denali" — the Great One. Mount McKinley is part of Denali National Park.

White-faced Mount McKinley looms above a Denali National Park road

THE ARCTIC NATIONAL WILDLIFE RANGE

The Arctic National Wildlife Range is one of Alaska's great natural wonders. It is the wilderness home of **caribou,** Dall sheep, grizzly bears, wolves and birds. The Range protects 13,000 square miles of wild Arctic lands in the northeast corner of Alaska.

Part of this **refuge** for wildlife is the Brooks Range of mountains. Another part is the sloping plain that separates the mountains from the Beaufort Sea.

The Arctic National Wildlife Range in northeast Alaska protects caribou and other wildlife

LAND OF THE MIDNIGHT SUN

For Alaska's visitors especially, sunshine at midnight is a wonder. In its northernmost villages, Alaska is the Land of the Midnight Sun.

Because of the Earth's angle toward the sun, northern lands enjoy long summer days. At the town of Barrow, between May 10 and August 1 the summer sun dips but never sets.

In mid-winter, though, the sun never rises on Barrow and the rest of the Northern world.

Glossary

caribou (KARE uh boo) — large, northern cousins of deer, found in large herds; wild reindeer

musher (MUH shur) — the person who guides sled dogs along a trail

pod (PAHD) — a group of animals together, especially sea animals

refuge (REH fewj) — a safe place; an area overseen by the U.S. Fish and Wildlife Service for the protection of certain wild animals

sea level (SEE LEHV uhl) — the same height, or level, as the sea

INDEX